Emotional Fitness Easy Guide for Beginners

Establishing Personal Emotional Fitness Goals

By

Ronan Albert

Copyright@2023

Table of Contents

CHAPTER 1
Introduction

1.1 Understanding Emotional Fitness

Emotional fitness is a multifaceted concept that pertains to an individual's ability to effectively recognize, understand, manage, and navigate their emotions in a healthy and constructive manner. Much like physical fitness, which involves strengthening and conditioning the body, emotional fitness focuses on enhancing emotional well-being and resilience.

At its core, emotional fitness involves self-awareness, which is the foundation for emotional intelligence.

This self-awareness allows individuals to identify and comprehend their emotions as they arise. It goes beyond just recognizing whether you are happy, sad, or angry; it involves understanding the nuances of your emotional responses, the triggers that influence them, and the impact they have on your thoughts, behaviors, and relationships.

Emotional fitness also encompasses the capacity to manage emotions effectively. This means being able to regulate and modulate emotional reactions to various situations, preventing them from overwhelming or controlling your actions. It involves the development of coping strategies, such as relaxation techniques, mindfulness practices, and problem-solving skills, to handle emotional challenges constructively.

Moreover, emotional fitness extends to building resilience. Resilience enables individuals to bounce back from setbacks, stressors, and adversity. It involves adapting to change, learning from experiences, and developing a mindset that views challenges as opportunities for growth rather than insurmountable obstacles.

understanding emotional fitness is about recognizing the importance of emotional intelligence, self-awareness, emotion management, and resilience in leading a balanced and fulfilling life. It's a vital aspect of overall well-being that can positively impact every facet of one's personal and professional life.

1.2 Who Can Benefit from This Guide

This guide on emotional fitness is designed to be inclusive and beneficial to a wide range of individuals, regardless of their age, background, or current emotional state. Here's a breakdown of who can benefit from this guide:

1. **Beginners:** As indicated in the title, this guide is specifically tailored for beginners. If you're new to the concept of emotional fitness or just starting your journey toward greater emotional well-being, this guide will provide you with a solid foundation and practical tools to get started.

2. **Young Adults and Students:** Adolescence and young adulthood are periods of significant

emotional development and
change. This guide can be
immensely helpful for young
adults and students who are
navigating the challenges of
school, relationships, and personal
growth.

3. **Professionals:** Emotional fitness is
increasingly recognized as a
critical skill in the workplace.
Professionals in any field can
benefit from this guide to enhance
their emotional intelligence,
improve communication, and
manage workplace stress
effectively.

4. **Parents and Caregivers:**
Understanding emotional fitness is
essential for parents and caregivers
as it can help them foster
emotional intelligence in children
and provide a nurturing

environment. This guide offers insights into how to support emotional development in children.

5. **Individuals Facing Stress or Life Transitions:** Whether you're dealing with significant life changes, like a career shift or a breakup, or facing high levels of stress, this guide can provide strategies and techniques to manage emotions during challenging times.

6. **Those Seeking Personal Growth:** Emotional fitness is not just about addressing problems; it's also about personal growth and self-improvement. If you're interested in becoming a more emotionally aware and resilient individual, this guide offers a roadmap for continuous development.

7. **Anyone Interested in Mental Health and Well-being:** Emotional fitness is closely linked to mental health and overall well-being. Anyone interested in maintaining good mental health and leading a fulfilling life can benefit from the insights and practices shared in this guide.

1.3 Why Emotional Fitness Matters

Emotional fitness is not a luxury; it's a necessity for leading a healthy, fulfilling, and successful life. Here's why emotional fitness matters:

1. **Improved Mental Health:** Emotional fitness is closely tied to mental health. Developing emotional intelligence and

resilience can reduce the risk of mental health issues such as depression, anxiety, and stress-related disorders.

2. **Enhanced Relationships:** Effective communication, empathy, and emotional regulation are vital for building and maintaining healthy relationships. Emotional fitness can lead to better connections with family, friends, and colleagues.

3. **Increased Productivity:** In the workplace, emotional fitness can lead to higher productivity, better teamwork, and improved leadership skills. It also helps individuals handle workplace stress and conflict more effectively.

4. **Better Decision-Making:** Emotional fitness empowers individuals to make informed decisions by considering their emotions and the emotions of others. It reduces impulsive reactions and fosters sound judgment.

5. **Resilience in Adversity:** Life is filled with challenges and setbacks. Emotional fitness equips individuals with the tools to bounce back from adversity, adapt to change, and grow stronger through difficult experiences.

6. **Enhanced Physical Health:** There is a strong link between emotional well-being and physical health. High levels of stress and unresolved emotions can contribute to health problems.

Emotional fitness can reduce these risks.

7. **Personal Fulfillment:** Emotional fitness contributes to a sense of personal fulfillment and happiness. It enables individuals to pursue their passions, set and achieve meaningful goals, and lead a purpose-driven life.

8. **Empowerment:** Emotional fitness puts individuals in control of their emotions, rather than being controlled by them. It empowers people to navigate life's challenges with confidence and grace.

In essence, emotional fitness is a fundamental aspect of holistic well-being. It equips individuals with the emotional tools and resilience needed to thrive in a complex and ever-changing world. This guide aims to

empower individuals to take charge of
their emotional fitness, recognizing
that it is a valuable investment in their
overall quality of life.

CHAPTER 2

The Basics of Emotional Fitness

2.1 Defining Emotional Fitness

Emotional fitness refers to an individual's ability to effectively manage, understand, and respond to their emotions and the emotions of others. It encompasses a range of skills and qualities that enable individuals to navigate the complexities of their emotional experiences in a healthy and adaptive way. Just as physical fitness involves maintaining and strengthening the body, emotional fitness involves nurturing and enhancing emotional well-being.

At its core, emotional fitness involves self-awareness, self-regulation, empathy, and interpersonal skills. Individuals who are emotionally fit are better equipped to handle stress, communicate effectively, and build meaningful relationships. Emotional fitness also includes the capacity to bounce back from setbacks, maintain a positive outlook, and adapt to changes with resilience.

2.2 Emotional Intelligence Explained

Emotional intelligence (EI) is a central component of emotional fitness. It refers to the ability to recognize, understand, manage, and utilize one's own emotions as well as the emotions of others. EI is often divided into several key domains:

1. **Self-Awareness:** This involves recognizing and understanding your own emotions, including their triggers, strengths, and limitations. It's about being in tune with your emotional landscape and acknowledging how your feelings influence your thoughts and behaviors.

2. **Self-Regulation:** This refers to the ability to manage and regulate your emotions in various situations. It involves avoiding impulsive reactions, controlling negative emotions, and responding thoughtfully to challenges.

3. **Motivation:** Emotional fitness also involves being driven by

intrinsic motivation rather than external factors. This means setting and pursuing goals that align with your values and passions, which can lead to a deeper sense of fulfillment.

4. **Empathy:** Empathy is the ability to understand and share the feelings of others. It involves actively listening, considering others' perspectives, and responding with compassion.

5. **Social Skills:** These skills include effective communication, conflict resolution, and the ability to build and maintain positive relationships. Socially skilled individuals are adept at navigating social dynamics and working collaboratively.

Emotional intelligence is not fixed; it can be developed and improved over time through self-awareness, practice, and learning from experiences. Developing emotional intelligence is a critical aspect of enhancing emotional fitness.

2.3 The Connection Between Emotions and Physical Health

The mind-body connection is a well-established concept, and the relationship between emotions and physical health is a significant aspect of emotional fitness. Research has shown that there is a strong interplay between emotional well-being and physical well-being. Here are some ways in which emotions impact physical health:

1. **Stress and the Body:** Chronic stress, often fueled by unmanaged emotions, can lead to a range of physical health issues, including cardiovascular problems, digestive disorders, and a weakened immune system.

2. **Inflammation:** Negative emotions, such as anger, resentment, and anxiety, can trigger inflammatory responses in the body. Chronic inflammation is associated with various diseases, including heart disease and autoimmune conditions.

3. **Immune System Function:** Positive emotions and a healthy emotional state have been linked to a stronger immune system. People with higher emotional well-being tend to have better immune responses.

4. **Pain Perception:** Emotions can influence how we perceive and experience pain. Negative emotions can amplify pain sensations, while positive emotions can help alleviate pain to some extent.

5. **Lifestyle Choices:** Emotional well-being can impact lifestyle choices, such as diet, exercise, and sleep. Individuals with higher emotional fitness are more likely to make healthier choices that contribute to their overall well-being.

6. **Longevity:** Research suggests that individuals with strong emotional well-being tend to live longer and experience a better quality of life in their later years.

Recognizing the connection between emotions and physical health underscores the importance of emotional fitness as a holistic approach to well-being. By cultivating emotional intelligence, managing emotions effectively, and nurturing a positive emotional state, individuals can contribute to their physical health and overall vitality.

CHAPTER 3
Self-Awareness

3.1 Recognizing Your Emotions

Self-awareness is the cornerstone of emotional fitness and the key to understanding and managing your emotions. Before you can effectively navigate your emotional landscape, you must first recognize and identify your emotions. This involves being attuned to the subtle shifts in your feelings, acknowledging them without judgment, and understanding their triggers.

Emotions are diverse and complex, ranging from the basic emotions like joy, sadness, anger, and fear to more nuanced feelings like envy, gratitude, and guilt. By developing the ability to accurately identify and label your emotions, you empower yourself to respond to them in a healthier and more constructive way.

Mindfulness is a powerful practice that can aid in recognizing emotions. It involves being present in the moment without judgment, allowing you to observe your emotions as they arise without becoming overwhelmed by them. By paying attention to your thoughts, bodily sensations, and feelings, you can gradually build a deeper understanding of your emotional landscape.

3.2 The Importance of Self-Reflection

Self-awareness goes beyond recognizing emotions; it also involves understanding the underlying causes and patterns that drive your emotional responses. Self-reflection is the process of introspectively examining your thoughts, feelings, and behaviors to gain insight into why you react the way you do.

Through self-reflection, you can uncover recurring themes, past experiences, and personal values that shape your emotional reactions. This awareness provides a solid foundation for personal growth and the development of emotional fitness. It allows you to make more intentional choices, respond thoughtfully to challenges, and align your actions with your values.

Self-reflection can be facilitated through practices like meditation, deep contemplation, and conversations with trusted friends or mentors. Regular self-reflection encourages a deeper understanding of your emotional triggers and empowers you to make positive changes in your life.

3.3 Journaling as a Tool for Self-Awareness

Journaling is a practical and effective tool for enhancing self-awareness and emotional fitness. It involves putting your thoughts and feelings into written words, allowing you to externalize your internal experiences. Here's how journaling can contribute to self-awareness:

1. **Emotional Expression:** Writing in a journal provides an outlet for expressing your emotions in a safe and nonjudgmental space. This can help you process intense emotions and gain clarity.

2. **Identifying Patterns:** As you write consistently, you may notice recurring patterns in your emotions and reactions. This awareness enables you to address these patterns and make positive changes.

3. **Triggers and Insights:** Through journaling, you can identify specific triggers that evoke strong emotional responses. This knowledge empowers you to prepare for and manage these triggers more effectively.

4. **Tracking Progress:** Journaling allows you to track your emotional journey over time. You can observe how you've grown, the challenges you've overcome, and the lessons you've learned.

5. **Problem-Solving:** Writing about challenging situations and your emotional reactions can help you explore different perspectives and brainstorm solutions. This can lead to better decision-making and coping strategies.

To make the most of journaling, set aside regular time for writing, choose a comfortable setting, and write freely without worrying about grammar or structure. You can explore various journaling prompts, such as describing your day, reflecting on recent experiences, or jotting down your goals and aspirations.

self-awareness is a foundational skill
for emotional fitness, and recognizing
emotions, practicing self-reflection,
and using journaling as a tool are
effective ways to cultivate this skill.
By engaging in these practices, you
can develop a deeper understanding of
yourself, enhance your emotional
intelligence, and navigate your
emotions with greater insight and
balance.

CHAPTER 4
Managing Emotions

4.1 Strategies for Handling Negative Emotions

Negative emotions are a natural part of life, but how you manage them can greatly impact your emotional well-being. Here are some strategies for effectively handling negative emotions:

1. **Identify Triggers:** Recognize the situations, people, or circumstances that tend to trigger your negative emotions. Awareness of triggers can help you prepare and respond more intentionally.

2. **Practice Mindfulness:** Engage in mindfulness techniques to observe your negative emotions without judgment. Mindfulness allows you to distance yourself from your emotions and respond thoughtfully rather than reactively.

3. **Use Positive Self-Talk:** Challenge negative thoughts with positive and rational self-talk. Replace self-criticism with self-compassion and remind yourself of your strengths and past successes.

4. **Emotion Labeling:** Labeling your emotions accurately can help reduce their intensity. Instead of saying "I'm stressed," specify whether you're feeling anxious, overwhelmed, or frustrated.

5. **Express Emotions:** Find healthy ways to express your negative

emotions, such as talking to a friend, journaling, or engaging in creative activities. Expression can provide relief and prevent emotions from building up.

6. **Problem-Solving:** If your negative emotions stem from a specific issue, focus on finding practical solutions. Break down the problem into smaller steps and take action.

4.2 Cultivating Positive Emotions

Cultivating positive emotions can contribute significantly to emotional fitness and overall well-being. Here's how you can foster positive emotions:

1. **Practice Gratitude:** Regularly express gratitude for the positive aspects of your life. This practice

shifts your focus from what's lacking to what you have, promoting a positive outlook.

2. **Engage in Activities You Enjoy:** Participate in activities that bring you joy and fulfillment. Engaging in hobbies, spending time with loved ones, or pursuing interests can boost your mood.

3. **Practice Acts of Kindness:** Doing something kind for others can generate feelings of happiness and satisfaction. It also enhances your social connections and sense of community.

4. **Savor Positive Moments:** Take time to savor and fully experience positive moments. Whether it's a beautiful sunset or a heartfelt compliment, savoring intensifies positive emotions.

5. **Practice Positive Affirmations:**
   Use positive affirmations to
   reinforce a positive self-image.
   Repeat affirmations that align with
   your values and aspirations.

4.3 Breathing and Relaxation Techniques

Breathing and relaxation techniques
are effective tools for managing
emotions in the moment. They help
activate the body's relaxation
response, which counteracts the
physiological effects of stress and
negative emotions:

1. **Deep Breathing:** Practice
   deep, diaphragmatic breathing
   by inhaling deeply through
   your nose, allowing your
   abdomen to expand. Exhale

slowly through your mouth.
Deep breathing calms the
nervous system and reduces
tension.

2. **Progressive Muscle Relaxation:** This technique involves tensing and then releasing each muscle group in your body. It helps relieve physical tension and promotes a sense of relaxation.

3. **Mindfulness Meditation:** Engage in mindfulness meditation to anchor your attention to the present moment. This practice can reduce anxiety and increase your ability to manage your emotions.

4. **Guided Imagery:** Use guided imagery to visualize a calming

and serene place. Guided imagery can help shift your focus away from negative emotions and induce a state of relaxation.

5. **Box Breathing:** Inhale for a count of four, hold for a count of four, exhale for a count of four, and then pause for a count of four before inhaling again. This technique can help regulate your breathing and calm your mind.

Incorporating these strategies into your daily routine, you can develop a repertoire of tools for effectively managing your emotions. Remember that emotional fitness is an ongoing practice, and by cultivating these skills, you can enhance your ability to

respond to both negative and positive
emotions in a balanced and adaptive
manner.

CHAPTER 5

Building Resilience

5.1 Understanding Resilience

Resilience is a multifaceted and vital psychological trait that enables individuals to adapt, bounce back, and thrive in the face of adversity, challenges, and setbacks. It's the capacity to withstand, recover from, and grow stronger through difficult experiences. Resilience is not a fixed characteristic; it's a skill and a mindset that can be developed and honed over time.

Here are key aspects of resilience:

1. **Adaptability:** Resilient individuals are flexible and able to adjust to changing circumstances. They do not get stuck in negative patterns or dwell excessively on past failures. Instead, they view change as an opportunity for growth.

2. **Emotional Regulation:** Resilience involves the ability to manage and regulate emotions effectively. Resilient people acknowledge their emotions without being overwhelmed by them. They use coping strategies like mindfulness, deep breathing, or talking to trusted individuals to navigate emotional challenges.

3. **Problem-Solving:** Resilience is linked to problem-solving skills. Resilient individuals approach challenges with a solution-oriented

mindset. They break problems down into manageable steps and seek practical solutions.

4. **Optimism:** Maintaining a positive outlook, even in the face of adversity, is a hallmark of resilience. Resilient people believe in their ability to overcome challenges and have hope for a better future.

5. **Social Support:** Building and maintaining strong social connections is essential for resilience. Having a support network of friends, family, or mentors can provide emotional support and practical assistance during tough times.

6. **Self-Compassion:** Resilient individuals practice self-compassion, treating themselves

with the same kindness and understanding that they offer to others. They do not engage in harsh self-criticism, even when they make mistakes.

7. **Growth Mindset:** Resilience is closely related to having a growth mindset, which means believing that abilities and intelligence can be developed with effort and learning. This mindset fosters a willingness to embrace challenges as opportunities for growth.

8. **Learned Resilience:** Resilience is not solely an innate trait; it can be learned and developed throughout life. Experiences, coping strategies, and support systems all play a role in building resilience.

Resilience is not about avoiding or suppressing negative emotions; it's about facing them, learning from them, and using them as catalysts for growth. It's also about recognizing that setbacks are a part of life and can provide valuable lessons and opportunities for personal development.

resilience is the ability to adapt, endure, and grow stronger in the face of adversity. It's a dynamic quality that can be cultivated and strengthened through self-awareness, coping strategies, and a positive mindset. Building resilience is an essential component of emotional fitness and can empower individuals to navigate life's challenges with grace and determination.

5.2 Resilience-Building Activities

Certainly, here are some resilience-building activities that individuals can engage in to strengthen their ability to bounce back from adversity and thrive in challenging situations:

1. **Develop a Support System:** Building a strong support network of friends, family, or mentors is crucial for resilience. Spend time nurturing these relationships and don't hesitate to reach out for support when needed.

2. **Practice Self-Care:** Prioritize self-care activities that promote physical and emotional well-being. This includes getting regular exercise, maintaining a balanced diet, getting enough sleep, and

managing stress through relaxation
techniques like meditation or yoga.

3. **Set Realistic Goals:** Establishing
    achievable goals, both short-term
    and long-term, can help maintain
    motivation and provide a sense of
    purpose. Break larger goals into
    smaller, manageable steps to track
    progress and celebrate
    achievements along the way.

4. **Cultivate Optimism:** Foster a
    positive outlook by focusing on
    solutions rather than dwelling on
    problems. Challenge negative self-
    talk and practice reframing
    challenges as opportunities for
    growth.

5. **Learn from Setbacks:** Embrace
    failures and setbacks as valuable
    learning experiences. Analyze
    what went wrong, what could be

done differently, and use this knowledge to improve future efforts.

6. **Seek Professional Help:** If dealing with significant trauma or persistent emotional challenges, consider seeking the guidance of a therapist or counselor who specializes in resilience-building and emotional well-being.

7. **Mindfulness and Meditation:** Engage in mindfulness practices and meditation to cultivate emotional regulation and mental clarity. These practices can help you stay grounded and calm during difficult times.

8. **Express Gratitude:** Regularly express gratitude for the positive aspects of your life. This practice can help shift your focus from

what's lacking to what you have,
fostering a more positive mindset.

9. **Engage in Hobbies and Interests:** Dedicate time to activities and hobbies that bring you joy and fulfillment. These activities can serve as outlets for stress and sources of inspiration.

10. **Volunteer and Help Others:** Volunteering and helping others in need can provide a sense of purpose, increase feelings of self-worth, and strengthen your connection to your community.

11. **Practice Flexibility:** Develop adaptability by intentionally exposing yourself to new experiences and challenges. Step outside of your comfort zone to build resilience in the face of the unknown.

12. **Keep a Resilience Journal:** Maintain a journal where you record your experiences, challenges, and the strategies you've used to overcome them. Reflect on your progress and celebrate your resilience.

13. **Self-Compassion:** Treat yourself with kindness and self-compassion, especially during difficult times. Avoid self-criticism and practice self-care to nurture your emotional well-being.

14. **Connect with Nature:** Spending time in nature can have a calming and rejuvenating effect. Nature walks, hiking, or simply sitting outdoors can help you recharge and build resilience.

15. **Join Support Groups:** Consider joining support groups or

communities of individuals who have faced similar challenges. Sharing experiences and coping strategies with others can be empowering.

16. **Learn Stress Management Techniques:** Stress is a common challenge that tests resilience. Learn stress management techniques such as deep breathing, progressive muscle relaxation, or time management to reduce the impact of stress.

Resilience is a skill that can be developed and strengthened over time. It's not about avoiding challenges but about developing the capacity to navigate them effectively and emerge stronger. Incorporating these activities into your life can help you build and maintain resilience, enhancing your overall emotional fitness.

5.3 Developing a Resilient Mindset

Developing a resilient mindset is crucial for building and sustaining resilience. A resilient mindset involves cultivating a set of beliefs, attitudes, and thought patterns that enable you to navigate adversity and setbacks with strength and adaptability. Here are key strategies for developing a resilient mindset:

1. **Embrace Challenges as Opportunities:** Train yourself to view challenges as opportunities for growth and learning rather than insurmountable obstacles. When faced with a difficult situation, ask

yourself what you can learn from it and how it can contribute to your personal development.

2. **Develop a Growth Mindset:** Adopt a growth mindset, which is the belief that abilities and intelligence can be developed through effort and learning. This mindset fosters a willingness to persevere, take on challenges, and see failures as stepping stones to success.

3. **Cultivate Self-Compassion:** Be kind and compassionate to yourself, especially during tough times. Avoid self-criticism and negative self-talk. Treat yourself with the same care and understanding that you would offer to a friend facing a similar situation.

4. **Maintain Perspective:** Practice keeping life's challenges in perspective. Avoid catastrophic thinking, where you magnify problems out of proportion. Remind yourself of past challenges you've overcome and the strengths you possess.

5. **Develop Resilient Thinking Patterns:** Challenge and reframe negative thinking patterns. For example, instead of thinking, "I can't do this," shift your perspective to, "This is difficult, but I can learn and adapt."

6. **Cultivate Optimism:** Cultivate an optimistic outlook by focusing on positive aspects of situations. Look for silver linings and potential solutions rather than dwelling on the negative aspects.

7. **Stay Adaptable:** Be open to change and willing to adapt to new circumstances. Avoid rigid thinking and embrace flexibility in your approach to challenges.

8. **Build Emotional Awareness:** Develop a deep understanding of your emotions and how they influence your thoughts and behaviors. Recognize when you are experiencing stress, fear, or frustration, and practice emotional regulation techniques to manage these feelings effectively.

9. **Learn from Setbacks:** Rather than dwelling on failures, actively seek the lessons they offer. Analyze what went wrong, what you can do differently next time, and how you can use this experience to improve.

10. **Set Realistic Expectations:** Maintain realistic expectations about yourself and others. Unrealistic expectations can lead to disappointment and decreased resilience. Understand that setbacks and mistakes are a natural part of life.

11. **Seek Support:** Don't hesitate to reach out to your support network when you need help. Resilience is not about facing challenges alone; it's about knowing when to seek assistance and support from others.

12. **Practice Patience:** Recognize that building resilience is a gradual process. Be patient with yourself as you develop these skills and gradually strengthen your resilient mindset.

13. **Visualize Success:** Visualize yourself overcoming challenges and achieving your goals. This can boost your confidence and motivation, making it easier to persevere through difficult times.

14. **Celebrate Small Wins:** Acknowledge and celebrate your small victories and achievements. These moments of success can provide motivation and reinforce your belief in your ability to overcome challenges.

15. **Maintain a Sense of Purpose:** Cultivate a sense of purpose and meaning in your life. Knowing your values and what you are working toward can provide direction and motivation during challenging times.

Actively practicing these strategies, you can foster a resilient mindset that serves as a foundation for building and maintaining resilience in the face of life's inevitable ups and downs. Developing a resilient mindset empowers you to not only endure adversity but to thrive and grow stronger as a result.

CHAPTER 6

Nurturing Relationships

6.1 Emotional Fitness in Relationships

Emotional fitness plays a pivotal role in maintaining healthy, fulfilling relationships. When individuals are emotionally fit, they are better equipped to engage in meaningful connections, communicate effectively, and navigate the complexities of interpersonal dynamics. Here's why emotional fitness is essential in relationships:

1. **Empathy and Understanding:** Emotional fitness fosters empathy,

the ability to understand and share the feelings of others. Empathetic individuals are more attuned to the emotions of their partners, which enhances understanding and connection.

2. **Effective Conflict Resolution:** Emotional fitness equips individuals with the skills needed to manage conflicts constructively. It helps them remain calm, express their feelings and needs clearly, and listen actively to their partner's perspective.

3. **Stress Reduction:** A key aspect of emotional fitness is stress management. When individuals can manage their own stress, they're less likely to project it onto their partners or react negatively to their partner's stress.

4. **Open Communication:**
Emotional fitness encourages open
and honest communication. It
empowers individuals to express
their emotions and needs, fostering
a safe and supportive environment
for discussions.

5. **Resilience in Relationships:**
Resilience, a component of
emotional fitness, is vital in
maintaining healthy relationships.
Resilient individuals bounce back
from relationship challenges, learn
from them, and continue to nurture
their connections.

6. **Healthy Boundaries:** Emotional
fitness helps individuals establish
and maintain healthy boundaries in
their relationships. This ensures
that each person's emotional needs
are respected and honored.

7. **Building Trust:** Emotional fitness contributes to building and maintaining trust in relationships. Trust is the foundation of strong and lasting connections.

6.2 Communication Skills

Effective communication is a cornerstone of nurturing relationships. It involves not only speaking but also listening actively and empathetically. Here are key communication skills that can enhance relationships:

1. **Active Listening:** Pay full attention to what your partner is saying without interrupting or formulating your response in your mind. Show that you understand

by using verbal and nonverbal
cues.

2. **Empathetic Responses:** Respond
   to your partner's emotions with
   empathy. Acknowledge their
   feelings and validate their
   experiences, even if you don't
   agree.

3. **Nonverbal Communication:** Be
   aware of your body language, tone
   of voice, and facial expressions.
   Nonverbal cues can convey as
   much, if not more, than words.

4. **Clarity and Transparency:**
   Express your thoughts and feelings
   clearly and honestly. Avoid vague
   or passive-aggressive
   communication that can lead to
   misunderstandings.

5. **Respectful Disagreements:**
   Disagreements are natural in any

relationship. When conflicts arise, address them respectfully, focusing on the issue at hand rather than resorting to personal attacks.

6. **Use "I" Statements:** Frame your thoughts and feelings with "I" statements to express yourself without blaming or accusing your partner. For example, say, "I feel hurt when..." instead of "You always..."

7. **Ask Open-Ended Questions:** Encourage open and meaningful discussions by asking open-ended questions that require more than a simple "yes" or "no" response.

8. **Practice Patience:** Give your partner time to express themselves fully, and avoid rushing to solutions. Sometimes, simply

listening and offering emotional support is what's needed.

9. **Mindful Communication:** Engage in mindful communication by being fully present in the moment. Avoid distractions and focus on the person you are communicating with.

10. **Feedback and Check-Ins:** Regularly check in with your partner about how the relationship is going. Provide constructive feedback and be open to receiving it as well.

11. **Conflict Resolution Skills:** Learn and apply conflict resolution techniques, such as compromising, finding common ground, and seeking win-win solutions.

12. **Appreciation and Gratitude:** Express appreciation and gratitude

toward your partner for their contributions to the relationship. Positive reinforcement strengthens connections.

Effective communication is a skill that can be developed and refined over time. By honing these communication skills and integrating them into your relationships, you can create an environment of trust, understanding, and emotional support, fostering healthier and more fulfilling connections with those you care about.

6.3 Conflict Resolution and Emotional Fitness

Conflict resolution is a critical aspect of maintaining healthy relationships, and it's closely intertwined with emotional fitness. Emotional fitness equips individuals with the skills and mindset needed to address conflicts in a constructive and empathetic manner. Here's how conflict resolution and emotional fitness are interconnected:

1. **Emotional Regulation:** Emotional fitness involves the ability to manage and regulate your emotions effectively. When conflicts arise, individuals with emotional fitness can stay calm and composed, avoiding emotional outbursts that can escalate the situation.

2. **Empathy and Understanding:** Emotional fitness fosters empathy, which is essential in conflict resolution. Empathetic individuals can see the situation from the other person's perspective, understand their feelings and needs, and

approach the conflict with greater
sensitivity.

3. **Active Listening:** Emotional
fitness encourages active listening,
a crucial component of resolving
conflicts. Actively listening to the
other person's viewpoint shows
that you value their perspective
and are willing to engage in a
meaningful dialogue.

4. **Conflict Management Skills:**
Emotional fitness includes the
development of conflict
management skills, such as
assertiveness, negotiation, and
compromise. These skills enable
individuals to address conflicts in a
respectful and solution-focused
manner.

5. **Open and Honest
Communication:** Emotional

fitness promotes open and honest communication. When individuals can express their thoughts and feelings clearly and transparently, conflicts can be addressed more effectively, reducing misunderstandings and resentment.

6. **Conflict as an Opportunity for Growth:** Emotionally fit individuals often view conflicts as opportunities for personal and relational growth. They understand that addressing and resolving conflicts can lead to stronger connections and greater understanding between parties.

7. **Resilience in Conflict:** Resilience, a key component of emotional fitness, helps individuals bounce back from conflicts and learn from them. Instead of dwelling on the negative aspects of a conflict,

resilient individuals focus on the lessons it offers.

8. **Problem-Solving Skills:** Emotional fitness includes the development of problem-solving skills. When conflicts arise, emotionally fit individuals can analyze the issue, generate potential solutions, and work collaboratively to find resolutions.

9. **Empowering Dialogue:** Emotional fitness empowers individuals to engage in constructive dialogues that aim at finding common ground and mutually beneficial solutions rather than engaging in blame or criticism.

10. **Conflict De-escalation:** Emotionally fit individuals are skilled at de-escalating conflicts,

reducing tension, and creating an atmosphere where both parties feel safe to express their concerns.

Emotional fitness and conflict resolution are closely connected. Emotional fitness equips individuals with the emotional intelligence, communication skills, and mindset necessary to navigate conflicts effectively. By applying these principles and skills, individuals can resolve conflicts in a way that strengthens relationships, promotes understanding, and fosters personal and interpersonal growth.

CHAPTER 7

Setting Goals for Emotional Fitness

7.1 Establishing Personal Emotional Fitness Goals

Setting personal emotional fitness goals allows you to focus on specific areas of your emotional well-being that you would like to improve or develop. Here are some examples of personal emotional fitness goals:

1. **Enhancing Self-Awareness:**
   Goal: To become more aware of my emotions and their triggers. Action: Practice mindfulness meditation for 15 minutes daily to observe and label my emotions.

2. **Stress Management:** Goal: To develop effective stress management techniques. Action: Learn and practice deep breathing exercises and progressive muscle relaxation for 10 minutes each day.

3. **Emotional Regulation:** Goal: To improve my ability to regulate my emotions in challenging situations. Action: When faced with a stressful situation, pause for a moment, take a few deep breaths, and consciously choose a calm and measured response.

4. **Building Resilience:** Goal: To bounce back more quickly from setbacks. Action: When I encounter a setback, identify one lesson I can learn from it and one positive step I can take to move forward.

5. **Conflict Resolution:** Goal: To improve my communication and conflict resolution skills. Action: Enroll in a conflict resolution workshop or online course to learn practical strategies for resolving conflicts.

6. **Positive Thinking:** Goal: To cultivate a more optimistic outlook on life. Action: Start a gratitude journal and write down three things I'm grateful for every day.

7. **Nurturing Relationships:** Goal: To strengthen my relationships with friends and family. Action: Dedicate one day a week to spend quality time with a loved one, engaging in activities we both enjoy.

8. **Setting Boundaries:** Goal: To establish and maintain healthy

boundaries in my personal and professional life. Action: Create a list of my core values and use them as a guide to set boundaries that align with my values.

9. **Goal-Setting:** Goal: To set and achieve personal and professional goals. Action: Identify one specific goal I want to achieve and break it down into smaller, manageable steps with deadlines.

10. **Self-Compassion:** Goal: To be kinder to myself and reduce self-criticism. Action: Practice self-compassion by treating myself with the same kindness and understanding I offer to others.

7.2 Creating a Plan for Long-Term Emotional Wellness

While setting specific emotional fitness goals is essential, it's equally important to create a long-term plan for maintaining and improving your emotional wellness over time. Here's how you can create such a plan:

1. **Assessment:** Begin by assessing your current emotional well-being. Reflect on your strengths and areas that need improvement. Consider using tools like self-assessment questionnaires or seeking input from trusted friends or professionals.

2. **Goal Setting:** Set clear and achievable emotional fitness goals, as outlined in section 7.1. Ensure that your goals are specific,

measurable, and relevant to your overall well-being.

3. **Action Steps:** Break down each goal into actionable steps. Determine what daily, weekly, or monthly actions you need to take to work toward your goals.

4. **Resources:** Identify the resources and support you may need to achieve your goals. This could include books, courses, therapy, or support groups.

5. **Tracking Progress:** Establish a system to track your progress toward your goals. This could be as simple as keeping a journal or using a goal-tracking app.

6. **Adjustment:** Be open to adjusting your goals and action steps as needed. Life circumstances

change, and your emotional fitness plan should remain flexible.

7. **Accountability:** Share your goals with a trusted friend or mentor who can hold you accountable for your progress and provide support when needed.

8. **Self-Care:** Integrate self-care practices into your routine to support your emotional wellness. This includes activities like exercise, meditation, proper nutrition, and adequate sleep.

9. **Learning and Growth:** Commit to continuous learning and personal growth. Stay open to new ideas and strategies for improving your emotional fitness.

10. **Celebrate Achievements:** Celebrate your achievements, no matter how small. Acknowledging

your progress can boost your motivation and reinforce your commitment to emotional wellness.

Emotional fitness is an ongoing journey, and it's perfectly normal to face setbacks along the way. The key is to remain committed to your goals and prioritize your emotional well-being as an essential aspect of a fulfilling and balanced life.

7.3 Tracking Your Progress

Tracking your progress in emotional fitness is a vital part of personal growth and development. By monitoring your efforts and results, you can make informed adjustments to your goals and strategies. Here's how to effectively track your progress:

1. Define Clear Metrics:

- Start by defining specific metrics or indicators that are relevant to your emotional fitness goals. These metrics should be measurable and related to the specific areas of improvement you've identified.

2. Set Milestones:

- Break your long-term goals into smaller, more manageable milestones or checkpoints. These milestones act as progress markers along the way and make tracking easier.

3. Keep a Journal:

- Maintain a journal or diary dedicated to your emotional

fitness journey. Record your thoughts, feelings, and experiences related to your goals regularly. Note any challenges you encounter and how you respond to them.

4. Use Technology:

- Leverage digital tools and apps to track your progress. There are many apps designed for goal setting, habit tracking, and emotional wellness that can help you log your efforts and visualize your progress.

5. Create a Visual Chart or Calendar:

- Develop a visual representation of your goals and milestones. You can use a calendar, a chart, or a vision board to display your progress. This allows you to see your accomplishments at a glance.

6. Regularly Reflect:

- Schedule regular reflection sessions to review your journal entries and assess your progress. Reflect on what's working, what needs improvement, and any insights you've gained.

7. Seek Feedback:

- Solicit feedback from trusted friends, family members, or mentors who are aware of your goals. They can provide valuable insights and offer an external perspective on your progress.

8. Measure Emotional Indicators:

- Pay attention to your emotional indicators, such as your ability to manage stress, react to challenging situations, or maintain a positive mindset. Consider using self-assessment questionnaires or tools designed to measure emotional intelligence.

9. Celebrate Achievements:

- Celebrate your successes, no matter how small they may seem. Recognizing your achievements can boost motivation and reinforce your commitment to your emotional fitness journey.

10. Adjust Your Plan: - If you encounter obstacles or find that your initial strategies aren't yielding the desired results, be open to adjusting your plan. Modify your goals, action steps, or timelines as needed.

11. Stay Consistent: - Consistency is key to tracking your progress effectively. Make it a habit to log your efforts, review your goals, and take action toward improving your emotional fitness regularly.

12. Stay Patient and Compassionate: - Remember that personal growth takes time, and setbacks are a natural part of the process. Be patient with yourself, and practice self-compassion when you face challenges.

13. Stay Committed: - Stay committed to your emotional fitness goals even when progress may be slow or when you encounter obstacles. Consistent effort over time can lead to significant positive changes.

14. Adjust Your Goals: - As you achieve your milestones and grow emotionally, it's essential to adjust your goals to reflect your evolving needs and aspirations. Emotional fitness is an ongoing journey, and your goals should adapt to your changing circumstances.

Tracking your progress in emotional fitness not only helps you stay on course but also provides valuable insights into your personal growth and development. It allows you to make informed decisions and continuously improve your emotional well-being.

CHAPTER 8

Overcoming Common Challenges

8.1 Dealing with Stress and Anxiety

Stress and anxiety are common challenges in today's fast-paced world. Learning how to manage them effectively is essential for emotional fitness. Here are strategies to help you deal with stress and anxiety:

1. **Identify Stressors:** Begin by identifying the sources of your stress and anxiety. Understanding what triggers these feelings is the first step in addressing them.

2. **Practice Stress Reduction Techniques:** Engage in stress reduction techniques like deep breathing, progressive muscle relaxation, or mindfulness meditation. These practices can help calm your mind and relax your body.

3. **Exercise Regularly:** Physical activity is a powerful stress reducer. Incorporate regular exercise into your routine to release endorphins and reduce stress hormones.

4. **Maintain a Balanced Diet:** Eat a balanced diet rich in fruits, vegetables, whole grains, and lean proteins. Avoid excessive caffeine and sugar, which can exacerbate anxiety.

5. **Get Adequate Sleep:** Prioritize
quality sleep by establishing a
regular sleep schedule and creating
a calming bedtime routine. Lack of
sleep can significantly contribute
to stress and anxiety.

6. **Limit Exposure to Stressors:**
Whenever possible, limit your
exposure to stressors. This might
involve setting boundaries, saying
no to additional commitments, or
managing your time more
efficiently.

7. **Positive Self-Talk:** Challenge
negative or catastrophic thinking
patterns with positive self-talk.
Replace irrational fears with
rational, balanced thoughts.

8. **Seek Support:** Share your feelings
with trusted friends, family
members, or a therapist.

Sometimes, simply talking about your stress and anxiety can provide relief.

9. **Time Management:** Develop effective time management skills to reduce the pressure of tight schedules and deadlines. Prioritize tasks and break them into manageable steps.

10. **Set Realistic Expectations:** Be realistic about what you can achieve and accomplish in a given time frame. Avoid setting overly high or perfectionist expectations for yourself.

11. **Mindfulness and Relaxation:** Practice mindfulness to stay present and reduce rumination about past or future events. Incorporate relaxation techniques

into your daily routine to release tension.

12. **Limit Information Overload:** Reduce exposure to distressing news and social media if it contributes to your stress and anxiety. Set boundaries on screen time.

13. **Professional Help:** If your stress and anxiety become overwhelming or persistent, consider seeking professional help from a therapist or counselor who specializes in stress management and anxiety.

8.2 Coping with Change

Coping with change can be challenging, as it often brings uncertainty and disruption. Here are strategies to help you adapt and cope effectively:

1. **Accept Change as Inevitable:** Recognize that change is a natural part of life. Embrace the idea that change can lead to personal growth and new opportunities.

2. **Develop a Growth Mindset:** Cultivate a growth mindset, which sees challenges and change as opportunities for learning and development.

3. **Stay Flexible:** Be open to adapting to new circumstances. Flexibility allows you to adjust to change more gracefully.

4. **Break Change into Smaller Steps:** When facing significant change, break it down into smaller, manageable steps. Focus on what

you can control and take one step at a time.

5. **Maintain a Support Network:** Lean on your support network of friends, family, or colleagues for emotional support and guidance during periods of change.

6. **Seek Information:** Gather information about the change to reduce uncertainty. Understanding what's happening and why can help alleviate anxiety.

7. **Set New Goals:** In times of change, set new goals and adjust your plans as needed. This can provide a sense of purpose and direction.

8. **Self-Care:** Prioritize self-care during times of change. Maintain routines that provide comfort and

stability, such as exercise, a healthy diet, and adequate sleep.

9. **Mindfulness:** Practice mindfulness to stay grounded in the present moment, reducing anxiety about an uncertain future.

10. **Seek Professional Help:** If change leads to overwhelming emotions or difficulties in coping, consider seeking the guidance of a therapist or counselor to navigate the transition.

Change is a constant in life, and your ability to adapt to it is a valuable skill. By applying these strategies, you can better manage stress and anxiety related to change and approach new situations with resilience and a positive mindset.

8.3 Addressing Emotional Blocks

Emotional blocks can hinder personal growth and emotional fitness. These blocks often stem from past experiences, limiting beliefs, or unprocessed emotions. Addressing them is crucial for emotional well-being. Here's how to tackle emotional blocks:

1. **Self-Reflection:** Take time for self-reflection to identify any recurring patterns of emotional blocks in your life. Journaling can be an effective tool for this.

2. **Seek Professional Help:** If emotional blocks are deeply ingrained or related to traumatic experiences, consider consulting a therapist or counselor. They can provide guidance and therapeutic

techniques to help you address and overcome these blocks.

3. **Challenge Limiting Beliefs:** Identify and challenge any negative or limiting beliefs you hold about yourself or your abilities. Replace them with positive and empowering beliefs.

4. **Mindfulness and Meditation:** Practice mindfulness and meditation to become more aware of your thoughts and emotions. This awareness can help you recognize and release emotional blocks.

5. **Emotional Release Techniques:** Explore techniques like emotional release therapy, EFT (Emotional Freedom Techniques), or somatic experiencing to release pent-up emotions and traumas.

6. **Talk to Someone:** Share your feelings and experiences with a trusted friend or family member. Sometimes, talking openly about emotional blocks can provide relief and clarity.

7. **Visualization:** Use visualization exercises to imagine yourself breaking through emotional barriers and achieving emotional fitness.

8. **Self-Compassion:** Practice self-compassion by treating yourself with kindness and understanding as you work through emotional blocks. Avoid self-criticism.

9. **Artistic Expression:** Engage in artistic or creative activities, such as painting, writing, or music, to express and process your emotions.

10. **Set Small Goals:** Start with small, manageable goals to address specific emotional blocks. Gradually work your way toward larger goals as you build confidence.

8.4 The Importance of Consistency

Sustaining emotional fitness requires consistency and ongoing effort. Emotional well-being is not a one-time achievement but a lifelong journey. Here's why consistency is vital:

1. **Reinforcement:** Consistent practice of emotional fitness techniques reinforces positive habits and coping mechanisms,

making them more ingrained in your daily life.

2. **Adaptation:** Consistency allows you to adapt and adjust your emotional fitness strategies as needed. It helps you stay resilient in the face of new challenges.

3. **Long-Term Growth:** Emotional fitness is about continuous growth and improvement. Consistency ensures that you continue to evolve emotionally and maintain your progress.

4. **Stress Reduction:** Regular emotional fitness practices help reduce stress, making it easier to handle life's ups and downs with grace and resilience.

5. **Health Benefits:** Consistent emotional fitness can lead to improved physical health, as stress

reduction and emotional well-being are linked to better overall health.

6. **Stronger Relationships:** Emotional fitness practices, when maintained consistently, can lead to stronger, more fulfilling relationships with others.

7. **Emotional Stability:** Consistency in emotional fitness helps stabilize your emotional state, reducing mood swings and emotional volatility.

8.5 Integrating Emotional Fitness into Daily Life

Integrating emotional fitness into your daily life makes it a natural part of your routine. Here's how to do it:

1. **Create Rituals:** Develop daily rituals for emotional fitness, such as morning meditation, gratitude journaling before bed, or taking short breaks during the day to practice mindfulness.

2. **Set Reminders:** Use reminders on your phone or computer to prompt you to engage in emotional fitness activities, especially when you're just starting to establish these habits.

3. **Incorporate It into Existing Routines:** Integrate emotional

fitness into your existing routines. For example, practice deep breathing exercises while commuting or engage in self-reflection during your lunch break.

4. **Accountability:** Share your commitment to emotional fitness with a friend or family member who can help hold you accountable.

5. **Embrace Imperfection:** Understand that some days you may not have the time or energy for extensive emotional fitness practices. Embrace imperfection and do what you can in the given moment.

6. **Celebrate Progress:** Celebrate your consistency and the progress you make in your emotional fitness

journey. Positive reinforcement can boost motivation.

7. **Adjust as Needed:** Be open to adjusting your emotional fitness routines as circumstances change. Flexibility is key to integrating these practices into your daily life.

Emotional fitness is a lifelong endeavor, and it's normal to have ups and downs. By addressing emotional blocks, remaining consistent, and integrating emotional fitness into your daily life, you can cultivate emotional resilience and well-being that serves you in all aspects of life.

www.ingramcontent.com/pod-product-compliance
Lightning Source LLC
Chambersburg PA
CBHW070834260726
48660CB00005B/2049